CALLED

H(TO)PE:

The Story of
Sarah Koeppen,
founder of The Hope Box, Inc.

Sarah Koeppen

WESTBOW
P R E S S®
A DIVISION OF THOMAS NELSON
& ZONDERVAN

This book is a work of non-fiction. Unless otherwise noted, the author and the publisher make no explicit guarantees as to the accuracy of the information contained in this book and in some cases, names of people and places have been altered to protect their privacy.

WestBow Press books may be ordered through booksellers or by contacting:

WestBow Press
A Division of Thomas Nelson & Zondervan
1663 Liberty Drive
Bloomington, IN 47403
www.westbowpress.com
1 (866) 928-1240

Because of the dynamic nature of the Internet, any web addresses or links contained in this book may have changed since publication and may no longer be valid. The views expressed in this work are solely those of the author and do not necessarily reflect the views of the publisher, and the publisher hereby disclaims any responsibility for them.

Any people depicted in stock imagery provided by Getty Images are models, and such images are being used for illustrative purposes only.
Certain stock imagery © Getty Images.

Scripture quotations marked (AMPC) are taken from the Amplified Bible, Copyright © 1954, 1958, 1962, 1964, 1965, 1987 by The Lockman Foundation. Used by permission.

Scripture quotations marked (NIV) are taken from the Holy Bible, New International Version®, NIV®. Copyright © 1973, 1978, 1984, 2011 by Biblica, Inc.™ Used by permission of Zondervan. All rights reserved worldwide. www.zondervan.com The "NIV" and "New International Version" are trademarks registered in the United States Patent and Trademark Office by Biblica, Inc.™

Scripture marked (NKJV) taken from the New King James Version®. Copyright © 1982 by Thomas Nelson. Used by permission. All rights reserved.

ISBN: 978-1-9736-9579-0 (sc)
ISBN: 978-1-9736-9580-6 (e)

Library of Congress Control Number: 2020912041

Print information available on the last page.

WestBow Press rev. date: 8/6/2020

This story is about how God molded Sarah's heart – to make her heart break for what breaks His – creating the heart of The Hope Box!

Contents

CHAPTER 1

In the Beginning

I am the 4th and the 2nd. Being born into a large family means always being asked, "what number are you in the family?" I am the fourth child of twelve children and the second daughter. All of my siblings and myself are miracles! My mother was told she would never have children. My mom was a mighty prayer warrior and an amazing woman of faith. She cried out to the Lord to bless her womb and He did, so much so that after number twelve was born my father had a little *talk with Jesus* and told Him he needed to "*shut this down!*"

My birth was even more miraculous due to the fact that my mother took medications while pregnant with me (unbeknownst to her at the time) that were very dangerous and could cause birth defects. The doctors encouraged my parents to consider abortion since they had no way of knowing to what extent and effect the medications would have on me. You see during that time there was not a great way to see what was going on in the womb. Mom and Dad prayed and knew that I was meant to be born. To everyone's surprise, I was born healthy – with all ten fingers and all ten toes! The doctors and nurses kept counting them and checking me over thoroughly to make sure I was okay. Dad said that my birth was special. He said that the Holy Spirit's presence was so very strong in the delivery room. Dad was so overwhelmed that he went outside and praised the Lord, thanking Him over and over for protecting me and keeping me safe. I am so very thankful for my parents' faith and their choice to have me, and I am so very thankful to God for protecting me in my mother's womb. So many times we are afraid of what could happen that we forget that God is writing a really good story and all we need to do is have faith in the nothing, trusting that He will do what He said.

*"Before I formed you in the womb
I knew [and] approved of you [as
My chosen instrument], and before
you were born I separated and set
you apart, consecrating you; [and]
I appointed you as a prophet to the
nations."*

Jeremiah 1:5 AMPC

I grew up in Boulder, Colorado. My father, Walt, was a pastor of a church. My dad was the personification of the Father's heart. He made a commitment to our family that we were his first priority. Dad taught me how God loves His daughters, and how God loves me! I remember holding his hands and knowing without words his love for me.

My siblings and I always had access to him, no matter how busy he was with the church business, which drove his secretaries crazy at times. He was always there for me, even when he accidently left me by the side of the road! This happens sometimes when you have twelve children. One bright Sunday morning I was driving to church with my dad when we stopped at a red light. I jumped out of the car to spray my hair while looking into the window. The light turned green while I was fixing my hair, and you guessed it, my dad drove off leaving me standing there looking quite silly. A few moments later he came back around and said, "Sarah, I had a full conversation with you before I realized you were gone." I lost it laughing – it is the little things that get me.

One time, my dad delayed a sermon because he became aware that my brother and I were having a problem during a church service. Dad had one of the associate pastor's *stall* while he took my brother and me to his office. I was so upset and crying because my dad was not out there preaching because of us. I'll never forget what he said, "no sermon matters as much as the hearts of my children." He talked to us, prayed for us, and then went and preached his sermon. What a moment in my life to see the Father's heart for His children.

Growing up, I don't ever remember God not being a part of my life. Yes, I'm a P.K. (pastor's kid), and I am so thankful for my upbringing. That being said, I grew up in the church and began serving in various roles at an early age, from handing out bulletins to working in the kid's ministry, and everything in between. Being a P.K. meant moving around a lot. We moved to Texas and Indiana at different times. At one point, while living in Texas, my dad was in charge of performing baptisms. I went down every time we had a baptism service no matter what kind of clothes I had on. I was baptized seven times! I remember looking at my dad saying, "did you know that I am basically holy water because I was baptized seven times!" We both had a good laugh about that. I think I'm good now!

We returned to Colorado when I was twelve years old. During this period of time with God, I became aware at an early age that I would "know" things about other people. This got me into trouble sometimes because I'd say things that were not well received. Much like a prophet who has knowledge beyond themselves, I *knew* about people not because anyone told me about them – and that was not always good! (Example: So how long have you been cheating on your wife?) After a few red faces and my mom's eyes popping out, she realized that I had the gift of prophecy. Mom began teaching me that most of the time when God reveals things to you, it is for you to pray for that person or situation and not to be spoken aloud. She taught me to always ask the Lord what He wanted to do with what He was showing me. She taught me how to listen to the voice of God and obey. We studied the Old Testament prophets to help me understand what life was like being *God's mouthpiece*. I experienced some of those Old Testament prophet's troubles as a young child and teenager. Because of this ability, friends did not always want to hang around me. It was hard for them to keep something secret around me because they knew I was already aware of it even if they said nothing. I never judged them. It had more to do with them and not me, but it is funny how shame grips us.

I had encounters with demonic spirits. One afternoon while I was in town, a very tall man approached me and stood right in front of me. As I looked up into his eyes, I saw a demonic presence. The man said to me in a very deep voice, "we're watching you!" In that moment I asked God, "what do you want me to do?" The Lord told me to tell him that I was covered by the Blood of the Lamb and that he could not touch me, and then to turn and walk away from him and not look back. That's exactly what I did! I learned a valuable lesson that day; to always ask God what to do and to obey Him.

As I matured, God continued to use me both in the church and in the marketplace. My mother, Joyce, was a registered nurse and a midwife. She was an amazing mother, pastor, and friend. She was a gifted Bible teacher and counselor. She "mothered" many people and helped them change their lives. She also helped over five hundred women become mothers! Yes, my mom delivered over five hundred babies during her career! She allowed me to go along on many of these occasions to help assist in the births. Seeing the miracle of life put a great love in my heart of both mothers and babies. Mom made everyone around her feel so very loved. She made you feel understood, like you were her best friend. It was from my mom that I learned how to love others.

My mom was a strong woman; she experienced not only the loss of multiple babies through miscarriage, she also lost a full-term baby – their first son. This was an incredibly difficult time for both of my parents, but especially my mom. Mom and dad were living in Azores, Portugal, during this time, while Dad served in the Air Force. My dad's heart hurt so badly for my mother as she wept for her son! In desperation, my dad's heart was broken for his wife and was able to connect with a pregnant woman who could not raise her baby. They made a code word, "BABY," so when she had the baby they would know to come right away. Mom and dad were both so excited. They waited expectantly to receive the call – it finally came – their son was born! Yes, my mother and father had their son. God loves adoption! It is His master plan for all of us, to be born again into His family and be adopted.

> ***"Yet, to all who did receive Him, to those who believed in His name, He gave the right to become children of God - children born not of natural descent, nor of human decision or a husband's will, but born of God."***
> ***John 1:12-13 NIV***

CHAPTER 2

What Satan Meant for Evil God used for Good

Throughout my life, I have always felt close to God. His presence has always been near to me. There were times, though, in my life when I experienced hard things. No one is exempt from the enemy's attacks. Looking back over some of those experiences, I can see not only how the enemy tried to take me out in a variety of ways, but I can also see God's mighty outstretched hand protecting me!

As mentioned earlier, I am a miracle! Satan tried to take me out before I was even born through unforeseen dangerous medications taken during pregnancy. As I grew and developed, my mom began to realize that I did not learn like my other siblings. It was later discovered that I was dyslexic. Dyslexia is a learning disorder that causes reading difficulties with letters, words and other symbols. Although I was diagnosed with this disability, my mom never used that word in reference to me or my ability to learn. Mom homeschooled me and I am so very thankful for that decision. I never felt bad about myself because mom just let me know that I learned in different ways from others; she incorporated all of my five senses into my learning. She helped me to learn practical everyday skills needed for life. She always encouraged me and taught me how to find answers to questions I had, on my own. Memorizing scripture was a big thing in our house. If we wanted to do something like go to the movies with friends, instead of earning money by doing chores, we memorized scripture. Mom recognized that in order for me to memorize, I had to understand the *big picture* or context of the scripture. This enabled me to be able to memorize entire chapters of scripture! So, what could have been a major hurdle (dyslexia) put in my path to discourage me or keep me from all that God had for me, God turned it around for my good.

Another hurdle I've had to deal with since childhood is scoliosis. Scoliosis is a spinal deformity that causes unusual side-to-side curvature of the spine that can affect mobility and internal organ function. My condition is quite severe, which causes me a lot of pain at times (good thing I'm married to a chiropractor!), and at the birth of my first child, caused some complications which led to a near death experience. The delivery was very long and difficult, and after our first son was born, I slipped into unconsciousness. At that point, I woke up in Heaven. I've never experienced such complete and total peace. It was so beautiful! I was walking in a field of soft, lush, green grass. At one point I laid down in the grass and began making *snow angels* in it. I suddenly heard a voice saying, "Sarah, you have to go back, you have a son." I did not want to go back! I was told once more that I had to go back, at which point I woke up with a team around me. I remember my mom saying to me, "do not do that to me again!" I remember it took two weeks to recover from loss of blood and exhaustion, and again God was with me. He was protecting me and literally bringing me back to life!

A favorite family story that all my siblings, nieces, and nephews beg to hear is the story about when a rattlesnake curled around my body. Yes, you read that correctly – a rattlesnake! This happened when I was six years old while we were living in Texas on an old farm. One day my mother asked me to call the boys in for dinner. The farm was fairly large, several acres. I checked several of their favorite spots, the creek and the barn, but could not find them. Finally, I went and stood under this huge tree, which was a gathering place for us kids, and began to call for them. Suddenly, I heard the sound of rattling! A rattlesnake was right at my feet. Fear gripped me and I stood perfectly still. I did, however, begin to scream at the top of my lungs! My brothers, Jason and Theron, heard me. Then they saw the snake, which now was wrapping itself around me! Both of them came running but realized that they would not be able to get to me in time. By now, the snake was up to my waist! Theron looked down and saw an old rusty screwdriver lying in the dirt. He picked it up and was about to throw it when Jason warned him not to because he was worried he'd hit me instead. Theron responded, "I have to try and save her!" So, Theron threw that rusty old screwdriver with all of his might and he hit the snake – the screwdriver went through the mouth of the snake and knocked it off of me to the ground! Not only does the Lord close the mouths of lions, He also closes the mouths of snakes – with screwdrivers, no less!

Another attack of the enemy happened to me between the ages of seven and ten. I experienced trauma which left me feeling totally isolated and unable to share what happened, not even with my parents. I experienced deep rooted wounds, especially concerning my identity. If Satan can cause us to question God's love and who He says we are, then Satan is able to derail our calling and ultimately our destiny. This is why attacking identity is Satan's number one strategy of attack! Several years later, God did another miracle, releasing me from the pain and isolation experienced through the abuse. He healed me through a dream! In the dream, the trauma I experienced rolled across my mind's eye like scenes from a movie. I saw Jesus there with me. At first, I did not and could not look at Him, out of guilt and shame.

Even though it was not my fault what happened, I was still left with shame on me. I asked the Lord one day, "why did I feel shame over this?" He told me that the enemy comes to steal, kill, and destroy. He lies to you in hopes you will take on that shame, so you feel far from Jesus – Satan is a liar. Finally, I was able to look into Jesus' eyes and my spirit was flooded with love! He said to me, "Sarah, it's time, it's time" – I knew that He meant it was time for me to begin the healing process. I was able to share with my parents what happened. The Lord did a great healing in me, bringing me to a place of wholeness. He pulled me up, and all the lies and old wounds which Satan had meant to destroy me, Jesus filled me with the truth – the truth of who I was in Him; He filled me with His Spirit and deposited great joy in my heart!

> *"But as for you, you meant evil against me; but God meant it for good, in order to bring it about as it is in this present day, to save many people alive."*
>
> *Genesis 50:20 NKJV*

"And we know that all things work together for good to those who love God, to those who are the called according to His purpose."

Romans 8:28 NKJV

CHAPTER 3

God will Give You the Desires of Your Heart

Growing up, my greatest dream was to marry and to be a mom. My mom married when she was nineteen and I secretly dreamed of marrying at the same age! My other siblings had various aspirations – going off to college, starting their own business, etc., but for me, my heart was simply set on marrying and being a mom. From an early age I have loved babies. I guess helping my mother deliver so many fanned that flame. Children have always been my passion – I love their innocence and their freedom. I believe this is how God always meant us to be, not just in childhood. I believe the Father's heart beats especially fast for babies. Once during a church worship service while singing about heaven on earth, I posed the question to God, "what is heaven on earth?" At that moment, He directed my attention to my sister-in-law who was singing on the platform. She was very pregnant and close to her due date. God spoke to me and said, "***that*** is heaven on earth!" How miraculous is the mystery of life! Through The Hope Box, I have been able to help many babies, and in one sense I feel they are all my babies. God truly does give us the desires of our heart!

At the age of sixteen, I had a secret desire to go to Russia. My older sister was there at one point as a missionary in an orphanage and I wanted to go too! One day while helping with children's church, my dad received a note from a pastor about me; I had never met this pastor before. The note said, "tell your daughter Sarah, the Lord is going to give her the desires of her heart because she has delighted herself in Him." Not very long after that, a group contacted my dad saying that they were going to Moscow to work with orphans and asked if I would like to go. I was totally blown away! When I asked if he had called them, he said, "no, they called me," much to my surprise. I was able to raise the funds I needed and went to Russia a few months later. While there, I worked in an orphanage with the children and traveled into the city doing many outreach activities.

This was also when the Lord first shared with me that I would have a son. In a dream, a little boy ran up to me calling me mama and jumped into my arms. I had this dream two nights in a row. I was so confused! I was wondering, does God want me to be a single mom? The morning after the second dream, I asked God, "Lord if this is you, give me this dream again!" That night, I had the dream again but this time when the little boy ran up to me, I said to him, "go get your daddy," and he ran and jumped into my husband's arms. I woke up in a cold sweat! At this point in my life, I had given my heart and life totally to Jesus. I was going to spend my life dedicated to loving Jesus with all of my heart, soul, mind, and spirit. I had even talked to my friends about starting "The Christian Nun's Association." Marriage was not what I thought God had planned for me. As I prayed to God about all of this, He told me, "when you get back (from

Russia), I am going to give you away (as a bride)." I returned from Moscow on Christmas Eve. My family was singing "The Twelve Days of Christmas" at church (you know, since there were twelve of us kids), and as we were singing, Joel came in and saw me (he thought I was still in Moscow). He came straight towards the front of the church practically running; when my mom saw this, she turned to me and said, "honey, he's got it bad for you!"

Coffee anyone!? Not long after this, I asked Joel out on our first date, for coffee of course! Not one to beat around the bush, I told him immediately, "I know what you are thinking" to which he responded, "no, you don't!" We went back and forth a few times with this and then he said, "so, what am I thinking?" I boldly told him, "you want to date me and would like to marry me, so you need to talk to my dad and let's get this started!" He was pretty much blown away at that point and turned beet red. Not long after our first date, Joel *did* go see my dad and talked to him. This was my dad's rule for all of us girls – we had to have all boys who were interested in dating us meet with him so he could help us sort out the bad ones from the good ones. Dad did a pretty good job helping me that day. A few years later, Joel and I married. I was nineteen.

> *"Delight yourself also in the LORD, and he shall give you the desires of your heart."*
>
> **Psalm 37:4 NKJV**

CHAPTER 4

New Beginnings

Joel and I married twenty years ago on June 16, 2000. We were very blessed to have several mentors who helped us navigate our early days of marriage. From the start, we reached out to couples within our church who we respected and saw that they had strong relationships. We basically interviewed them, asking them what worked in their marriages and what didn't work. We were also very grateful to be able to meet with Bob and Carol Baker, who attended our church. The Bakers are veteran marriage educators who founded Marriage Foundations of Colorado. We were so fortunate to sit under their teaching. We gained many valuable tools through their guidance and teachings that helped us build a very solid foundation in our marriage. We began working with couples in the church, teaching classes, presenting at conferences and mentoring. We also started a ministry group within our church for newly married couples and couples with young families. We taught a lot about generational lines and marriage covenant. These were very fruitful years for us. God grew us so much and we were able to come alongside many couples and help them bring healing to their relationships and find new passion and intimacy in their marriages. Joel and I were the "sex-talk" couple. Since we were "newlyweds," we were deemed the experts or at least the guinea pigs! During this time, we also became parents to our four children. We had our first son, Austin, in 2001, our daughter, Hannah, followed in 2002. Next came Breydan in 2004, and then our son Avery in 2006. Then came Elijah in 2009, but more about him later.

Joel and I also began working with families in the local community. We were invited to join a marriage and family board in conjunction with the Department of Family and Children's Services (DFCS). We helped parents and families that were experiencing difficulties. We taught classes on family dynamics – everything from communication to discipline. Many of the parents and families we were involved with had themselves come from dysfunctional homes and did not have a grid for what *healthy families* looked like. Joel and I would have them over for dinners, modeling conversation and communication. We helped them develop parenting plans and followed up with them on a consistent basis. Through working with DFCS, we became aware of the many problems children faced in the system. We became aware that many children seemed to *fall through the cracks*. Due to the instability of parents, children were constantly moved from one county to another. Case workers often lost track of children/families, and services that had begun in one county were then halted. We worked with the board and in conjunction with surrounding counties in the area creating inter-county communications to help alleviate this problem.

God also used us to minister to young couples when we moved from Colorado to Georgia. Joel and I made the move to Atlanta, Georgia, in 2012 so that he could attend Life University and pursue his chiropractic career. It was tough leaving all of our friends and family in Colorado. We did not know a soul in Georgia, but God connected us with other young couples who had also moved to Georgia in order to go to Life University. We relied heavily on the marriage tools we learned and taught to others back in Colorado. Having a young family, moving across the country, and having a spouse in college are all stressful events. To have all three at one time, was very stressful, to say the least, especially as we navigated this new season. I remember driving into Georgia and asking the Lord, "why Georgia?" He began to tell me that we will be the answer to many people's prayers – I had no idea what that meant at the time.

We met other couples going through the same stressors as us and were able to share with them those same tools we used in Colorado. Although, we were no longer marriage mentors or ministers officially, God continued to use us in this capacity. We also made some life-long friends along the way!

> **"Therefore, a man shall leave his**
> **father and mother and be joined to his**
> **wife, and they shall become one flesh."**
> **Genesis 2:24 NKJV**

CHAPTER 5

Adoption Road

Joel and I have a history of adoption in both of our families; I have an older brother who was adopted, and Joel has a cousin who was adopted. Matter of fact, Joel and I are both adopted too – if you are a believer, you are adopted by God! God created adoption and it is His heart to adopt us into His family! Because adoption is God's desire, it also became our desire!

While living in Colorado, we prayed together, "teach us to love the way You love and care about what You care about." Not long after praying this prayer, a pregnant mother contacted me who was considering abortion, but who said she would deliver the baby, if Joel and I would adopt the infant. Joel and I talked and prayed and told her, "yes, we'd adopt your child." We were thrilled to be adding another child to our family. As we prayed for this baby, our hearts and spirits bonded with the baby. We fell in love! We went through the entire adoption process, which was lengthy. (During this time, I learned a lot about adoption!) Ultimately, the mother changed her mind and decided to keep her baby. This was a very hard time for both of us. We grieved the loss of this child. A few months later, to our shock and surprise, we had another pregnant mother reach out to us and ask us if we'd adopt her baby. We were not out looking for pregnant women, they found us! So, we went through the adoption process again and in the end, she decided to keep her baby after the delivery. To say we were crushed is an understatement. Our hearts were broken again, and we mourned the loss of another child. Why was this happening to us!?

A couple of months after losing baby number two, we had another pregnant mother contact us, asking if we would consider adopting her baby. At this point Joel was very concerned for me, as the previous two failed adoptions had taken such a toll on my heart. He asked me, "are you sure you want to go through this again?" My response to him was, "I don't know why, but I have to see this one through." The birth mother delivered and this time – we took home a beautiful baby boy! It was such an amazing time! I bonded immediately with him! I was so in love and so were all of his new siblings! But a week later, the birth mother changed her mind and we had to give the baby back to her. Heartbroken, I cried out to God, "***WHY!?***" He lovingly spoke to my heart and told me,

> "you asked to love the way I love and now you understand how I feel. This is how I feel when my children don't know me! When they walk away from me! I will never stop loving them just like you will never stop loving these children – whether you raise them or their birth mothers raise them – you now have a spiritual attachment to them and every time you pray for them, you speak as their spiritual mother! Your prayers are heard in

Heaven and each of these babies are
seen as your children."

Each of the babies we were to adopt, and we *lost,* were
boys. We have three spiritual sons that we continue to
pray for. Through this painful experience of three failed
adoptions, which I call *spiritual miscarriages*, I learned so
many lessons. I experienced the healing power of God's
love and I learned how much God loves His children.

> ***"For those who are led by the Spirit
> of God are the children of God. The
> Spirit you received does not make
> you slaves, so that you live in fear
> again; rather, the Spirit you received
> brought about your adoption to
> sonship. And by him we cry, Abba,
> Father. The Spirit himself testifies
> with our spirit that we are God's
> children. Now if we are children,
> then we are heirs – heirs of God and
> co-heirs with Christ, if indeed we
> share in his sufferings in order that
> we may also share in his glory."***
>
> ***Romans 8:14-17 NIV***

CHAPTER 6

Elijah: God's Promise of a Son

For two years following our third failed adoption, the Lord continued to bring healing to my heart. I knew in my heart that He had a plan and that all of the emotional ups and downs we'd been through were not in vain. Joel and I trusted the Father's goodness and we continued to walk in faith concerning all that had happened. As a Christ follower, we are not promised life without pain; in actuality, He assures us that we will experience it! However, He does promise to walk with us through our trials and to never leave us, and that is exactly what He did!

One morning, while showering and getting ready for the day, the Holy Spirit moved upon my heart. He told me, "Sarah, you have a son, he is older, and you need to pray for him to come home!" The Holy Spirit filled my heart immediately with an intense love and longing for this child. That evening after the kids went to bed, as Joel and I sat on the front porch enjoying a cup of tea, I shared with him what had happened. Understandably, Joel was concerned and questioned, "how could this even happen? Sarah, we're not even working with DFCS or an adoption agency – I don't know how this can happen!" My response to him was, "but God said, He is bringing our son home!" We began to pray fervently for our son. It is a strange feeling to know you have a child somewhere, but you have no idea where he is or even what he looks like. But through our prayers, God solidified in both of us, the hope of our son, who He was bringing into our family. Two weeks from the time of the Holy Spirit's announcement, an older lady whom I'd never met before, came up to me during church and said, "hi, you don't know me. My daughter was going to ask you to adopt her baby several years ago, but then changed her mind. Now she wants to know if you and Joel would take him." My immediate response was, "YES!" Of course, she had no idea what God had done in the previous weeks; what He'd spoken in my heart nor all of the prayers that we had prayed for this little boy. God is truly so amazing! We were excited beyond measure!

Shortly following this encounter with this young boy's grandmother, his mother, brought Elijah to our home. I will never forget that moment. His mother carried his little suitcase, car seat, and little bicycle up our driveway. He excitedly jumped out of the car and began playing immediately with our kids in the front yard. She called to him and he just turned to her and said, "bye". My heart hurt for her. I saw the love she felt for him in her eyes. Also, I saw the painful knowledge that she was unable to care for him.

Elijah had experienced a lot in his first three years. Due to his biological mother's life choices, he had experienced much emotional and physical trauma. Every day was a new challenge that we faced with love. Elijah was developmentally delayed, which is very common in children who have experienced trauma. Anger was his way of communication – screaming and hurling himself against the walls were daily occurrences. Panic attacks were common as well and we never knew what was going to trigger him in those early days. We knew we needed help for him as well as for us.

Elijah began seeing a play therapist. During our sessions, we both learned a lot. The therapist helped me to understand his behaviors and taught me ways to help him transition into our family. She realized that Elijah had not bonded with his biological mother, so she instructed me to hold him like an infant maintaining eye contact with him. An important part of infant brain development involves regular eye contact with its mother. Because this never happened she wanted to establish that connection for his continued brain development. She helped Elijah learn ways to cope with his feelings, and she gave us both tools to communicate with one another. Joel and I not only worked tirelessly with Elijah, but also with our other children as we sought to bring peace into the chaos which was our family.

Life settled into a new *normal* as we all adjusted. We began to see progress in Elijah's behavior. Each day he met goals and we felt like we were on the road to a healthy transition for all of us. Six months later, Elijah's biological mother showed up and took Elijah for two weeks. I felt like I'd been punched in my gut! How could this be happening!? The entire family was reeling.

After two weeks, and through unknown circumstances, Elijah ended up with his biological father – a man he had never known. Four weeks after Elijah was taken, we received a call from his biological father saying, "the police are after me, come get Elijah." We saw immediate setbacks in Elijah's behavior and communication skills. We were concerned for his physical and emotional health and future safety. We knew this was not good for him and realized that we had to do something legally to make sure this did not happen again. Although we had legal guardianship, it did not give us any rights beyond getting him medical help and enrolling him in school. We recognized that we needed to somehow get custody of Elijah in order to protect him from possible future harm.

During this time, I began to research laws concerning guardianship, custody, and abandonment. I became aware of a constitutional law that stated, if a child is in your home for six months or more, then you have standing to file for custody of that child. I read and reread this law. I called several different law firms and spoke to adoption lawyers asking them questions and determining if I'd interpreted the law correctly. Interestingly, many of the adoption lawyers were unaware of some of the things in the law but did assure me that I had interpreted it correctly. Next, I went to the courthouse to see about what forms I needed to complete. Elijah's aunt, who was very supportive of us having Elijah, helped me to complete the paperwork, giving me vital information when needed.

Custody papers were filed, and a court date was scheduled. I met with a family court facilitator while Joel waited in the hall. During this meeting, his mother stated she had no plans of taking Elijah back, but she did not want to terminate her parental rights. The family facilitator told us since we were not in agreement concerning custody we would have to go before a judge. While the court facilitator was talking, I realized neither of us had lawyers! Immediately, I began to have a conversation with God. "Lord, I don't know what I'm doing, and I've got to go before a judge. You said to do this, Lord, I need a lawyer now!" Coming back to reality I heard the family court facilitator say, "you'll have to go before the judge in the next fifteen minutes."

Entering the hallway in a frenzy, I found Joel and told him what was going on. "I've got to get a lawyer NOW!" To which he responded, "babe, you're not going to be able to get a lawyer in that short amount of time – he would not even have time to read up on the case." With the ferocity of a mother lion I told him, "WATCH ME!" For the next several moments I paced and prayed like a crazy woman in the hallway! A young man walked by me and the Holy Spirit said, "ask him," so I did! I asked if he was in family law? To which he answered, "no." He then pointed to the double doors in front of him and said, "but there are about twenty family lawyers in that room!" The next thing that happened could literally be a scene from a courtroom drama movie – I burst through the double doors and loudly announced, "My name is Sarah Koeppen and I need a lawyer, and I need one right now!" All twenty attorneys turned and looked at me incredulously. Then I heard, "Sarah, Sarah Roberson, is that you?" It was my childhood friend, Mark. He asked me what I needed, so I told him. He pointed to another lawyer standing beside him and said, "this guy right here will walk in with you." Which he did! He told the judge that his client (Joel and I) had standing, that I had constitutional law. Because it was an emergency hearing and this news complicated things the judge ordered that we'd reconvene the following day. Later that day we met with lawyers who explained to us how custody works, and they advised us to seek *sole* custody. They helped us prepare so that we would know what to say to the judge the following day. They continued to follow up with us throughout the proceedings and never charged us a dime!

The judge agreed that I had standing. As the court sees it, a child can only have two constitutional parents, usually a mother and father. Because she granted me standing, she had to remove his father's rights, making me Elijah's second parent. Because we were in dispute over custody, it appeared that his mother and I were "divorced" (since Elijah could legally only have two parents). Elijah became our legal son – having both constitutional rights and state rights. He could never be taken from us ever again. This whole process took about a year's time. With the input and support of several different lawyers, I was able to represent myself before the judge. We initially gained joint custody, then full custody and finally, sole custody.

During this time, I struggled with the decision, because I knew how hard this was for his mother and I felt bad about taking him away from her, but I had to concentrate on what was best for Elijah. Initially, she realized that it was the best decision for him. It was a rocky road for both of Elijah's moms! God was able to do a restorative work between us and we chose to have an open adoption, which means he can contact her if he chooses to and we keep in touch with his biological grandmother. We were very open with Elijah about his biological mom, letting him know how grateful we are for her. We let him know he could love her and love us too. This was very freeing for him; so many kids who are adopted feel they must

Sarah Koeppen

choose or feel *disloyal* over loving the other parent(s). We never made him feel he had to choose. I always told Elijah that he has two mom's, mommy number one because she had him –and we are so grateful – and mommy number two because we are raising him, and he can love us both.

As we navigated this new journey in our family, we definitely experienced a few "bumps" along the way. One of those bumps included a house fire. When Elijah was five, he accidentally set the house on fire. While he was in his room napping, or so I thought. He somehow found some matches and set a book on fire. Terrified, he tried to put it out hiding the charred and smoldering book under Avery's bed. The book continued to smolder and eventually caught fire along with Avery's bed! At first, he did not own up to what he'd done. Through some pretty good detective work on our part, along with the fire department we determined that he was the guilty culprit (there's just no explaining away burnt fingertips). It was a pretty traumatic experience for all of us; thankfully no one was physically injured. Our son, Avery, did experience some emotional trauma from the fire though, as his room was pretty much destroyed. He and Elijah shared a room, and this is where the fire started. Avery was most upset about the loss of his favorite blanket. This was the tipping point for him – he kept crying, "my blankie, my blankie!" We searched throughout the rest of the house hoping maybe it was in another room. We checked in all of the things that had been damaged or burned but could not find it. I told him I was so sorry and then I prayed with him and asked Jesus to return it to him. The following Sunday, we were in church and my sister Erin walked into the sanctuary carrying Avery's blanket! We'd not seen her in several weeks. This particular morning she'd opened her trunk and saw Avery's blankie, so she thought she'd bring it to him (she did not know about our conversation with Jesus)! I nudged Joel and pointed to my sister. Tapping Avery's shoulder, I told him to look – his eyes got so big and welled up with tears. He ran to Erin and his blankie, and literally began to dance; the rest of us were all crying. Avery was able to forgive his brother and we saw again, the goodness of God! He cares for us! He knows every minute detail of our lives, even down to the importance of our young son's beloved blanket!

Elijah is now fourteen years old and he is such an amazing kid! He is intelligent, handsome and very popular. He is everyone's best friend, and we are still teaching him about healthy boundaries with others. Because of all that he has been through, he has a heart of compassion and feels deeply for others, especially those like him who've gone through difficulties in their childhood. He has friends that are in foster care and also friends who are adopted. He is able to share his story with them and he encourages them to find joy.

Recently, Elijah has told us that he wants to change his last name to Koeppen (we did not want to change his name for him when he was younger; we wanted him to make that decision on his own). We told him, "absolutely, yes!" When we asked him why he wanted to change it, he said, "because I've earned it!" We are so proud of Elijah and are so very grateful to God for bringing us our promised son!

> *"Blessed is she who believed, for there will be a fulfillment of those things which were told her from the Lord."*
> **Luke 1:45 NKJV**

CHAPTER 7

Noah's Ark

As I look back over the years and the experiences Joel and I went through, I see now how God was orchestrating the creation of The Hope Box from the very beginning. Following the three failed adoptions and then Elijah coming into our lives, the Lord began birthing in my heart a desire to help at-risk mothers and their infants. I saw the great need and felt overwhelmed by it; however, I've also seen God's continued faithfulness through many things.

After our move to Georgia, God graciously gave me what I affectionately call "My Jesus Years." This was a season filled with healing, renewal and spiritual growth. Joel and the kids would all leave to go to school, and I would retreat to the porch and spend hours with the Lord.

One night, I had a dream. In the dream, my brother asked me if I was okay. I then told him, "my life will never be simple again." When I woke up, I asked the Lord what the dream meant. He told me that He was allowing me to grieve the fact that my life would never be uncomplicated from this time forward. Not long after this dream, I had what I call my "Noah's Ark" moment. I remembered what the Lord showed me in Colorado, that much like God gave Noah the "blueprint" for the ark, He gave me the blueprint for The Hope Box. During that time the Father began showing me the cry of his children, specifically the infants. God's plan was to change the way that mothers and infants are treated. He asked me to take the crisis out of each situation, breaking them down and making them work for mothers. His plan wasn't for us to be a part of an existing system, like DFCS, but to create safe places for mothers and children. He showed me that like spokes of a bicycle wheel we would reach out from a central core, our staff, like a hub, into the community through advocacy, education, changing legislation, and through partnering with local, state, and national organizations. The Lord showed me that I would start this in one area, but that the idea and concept would be adopted in many places – He showed me that I would be a mother to the nations. The dream seemed so large – all I ever wanted to do was to be a mother to my children. I didn't have a doctorate or esteemed education, why would God choose me for this dream? My first reaction to what God put in my heart was to laugh. I guess I was aptly named Sarah after Abraham's wife, who also laughed at God's plan for her! It seemed so huge, so impossible and so overwhelming that all I could do was laugh. Yet, in my heart, I knew that this was what God had destined me to do!

Blueprint Meets Reality

The Hope Box is a wheel with inner connected spokes that reach out into the local community and beyond. We are governed by a board that the Lord helped me hand pick. This group gives me great wisdom and counsel in all The Hope Box decisions, and I am forever grateful for their willingness to partner with God and what He is doing through The Hope Box.

Within this circle, is the Hope Box staff. Next, we have hundreds of volunteers that assist us in rescues and programs.

The Hope Box works as an advocacy group for at-risk mothers and infants. We assist mothers and equip them to make life decisions concerning themselves and their children. We have linked arms with other nonprofit organizations and work together to bring needed resources to mothers who choose to parent their children. From needed goods and materials, housing, assistance with completing necessary forms to receive aid from the government and other institutions, and everything else in between. The Hope Box works tirelessly to ensure that at-risk infants receive the care needed to thrive. When mothers decide not to parent their infants, we come alongside them and help them understand their legal rights and the various choices they may make concerning their infants.

The Hope Box is also an educational advocate for safe haven laws and training of those who are directly and indirectly impacted by this law. This includes training fire department personnel, police personnel, hospital employees, health department personnel and middle and high school students and staff.

The Hope Box works as a legislative advocate, connecting with local and state officials concerning the needs of at-risk mothers and infants. We advocate for laws to help protect them by continually bringing the pressing issues of child abandonment and abuse before those elected and appointed officials to make them aware – with hope that they will eventually help alleviate this issue in our state. Another goal of The Hope Box is to help establish better communication between the various entities that work with at-risk mothers and infants and improve overall services for them.

Finally, The Hope Box continually works to understand all pertinent laws both within our state and other states that affect at-risk mothers and infants, so that we may continually advocate and educate with the highest degree of understanding of those laws.

Our mission is to rescue and assist at-risk babies ages three and under by working with Georgia legislators, public safety professionals, medical personnel, and adoption professionals and by addressing the issue of infant abandonment. Our vision is to eliminate infant abandonment, neglect and abuse and to help infants connect with forever families where they can be physically, spiritually, and emotionally nurtured.

So, there is the ark!

> *"Many are the plans in a person's heart, but it is the LORD'S purpose that prevails."*
>
> **Proverbs 19:21 NIV**

CHAPTER 8

Building The Hope Box

"If you build it, they will come." This line from *Field of Dreams*, so aptly describes how The Hope Box went from a dream to a reality! Following the "Noah's Ark" moment, God brought a woman into my life who was a mutual friend of some friends from church. Over coffee, we shared with one another about our lives, our families and our hopes and dreams. There was an instant connection between us, and our friendship quickly developed. As I shared with her my vision of The Hope Box, her immediate response was, "I can help you get started!" God gave me the dream for The Hope Box and Tiffany gave me my *YES*.

We began meeting weekly together and brainstorming about the people we would need to have on our team and board. Because of all I had experienced with the adoption process with Elijah, I knew we'd need a district attorney on the board. During this time, I met a young nursing student who had recently moved to Atlanta to attend college. I began mentoring her and she knew of a district attorney, from her hometown, that had just moved to the Atlanta area. He was involved with a nonprofit in their hometown city in which they had served together. God is so good about making divine connections! She introduced me to him, and he helped us develop The Hope Box. From there Sai, my mentee and nursing student, connected me with members of the Kennesaw State University (KSU) Faculty. Over the course of several months we met with human resource professors, professors of nursing, as well as doctors as they helped us *flush* out The Hope Box blueprint. We were able to ask many questions concerning Georgia laws and medical mandates surrounding infant abandonment. Through this divine connection, we were given favor with KSU and did several presentations about infant abandonment with their nursing students. One professor even included us in one of her research books, which was eventually published and is now used in KSU's nursing program. God's favor was definitely upon us!

Another *chance* encounter happened one day while Sai was sitting in a coffee shop studying. At one point, I called her, and we were discussing The Hope Box. Unbeknownst to her, a lawyer who worked for a very prominent Atlanta law firm was sitting near her and overheard some of our conversation. He later struck up a conversation with her and from this *chance* encounter, we received free legal assistance in the establishment of The Hope Box as a 501(c)3 nonprofit organization! He also worked with children who had been sexually abused and trafficked which opened up a door for us to gain more knowledge and understanding concerning the trafficking of infants – something that I had been unaware of before then.

God provided for our every need, sometimes instantaneously! The team would meet to discuss our next steps and pray asking God to provide and He did, time after time! We were so encouraged and excited by all that He was doing. God strategically brought many different people into my path that had specific skill sets that helped us launch The Hope Box. I am so grateful to them for coming alongside me in those early years! From nursing students, to district attorneys, to politicians and more, all of them came together and said, "YES, this is possible!"

> *"...being confident in this, that he who began a good work in you will carry it on to completion until the day of Christ Jesus."*
>
> **Philippians 1:6 NIV**

CHAPTER 9

The Hope Box: Dream Becomes Reality

In late 2014, The Hope Box was launched! We had determined the launch would be in 2015, but the Lord had different plans. The original intent of The Hope Box was to have actual boxes located throughout the state so that mothers could relinquish their infants in them, no questions asked and no threat of prosecution. This was an idea that originated hundreds of years ago in Europe. As we researched this idea, we became aware of many other issues surrounding infants – one of them being *boarder babies*. No, these are not babies living on the borders of our country! They are babies that are being boarded in hospitals that are not allowed to go home, not due to medical reasons. Some of those reasons include legal issues of parents, concern that parents cannot or will not care for the infant, or homelessness. It came to our attention that in our local hospitals there are as many as twenty-five to fifty babies being boarded at any one time. These infants, though technically under the jurisdiction of the Department of Family and Children's Services, are not being adopted. During this time, the infants are being cared for by nurses in hospitals, as best as they are able to while also caring for sick infants. Babies may be in the hospital for months until foster families are found. Research shows the great importance of early bonding of infants and the detrimental effects when this does not occur. Not only are there cognitive delays or impairments, but also social and emotional delays or impairments. We felt called to advocate for these babies who deserve and need forever homes. We offered our services to DFCS to assist them in any way we could to help speed up the process of getting babies into forever homes. We also continued working to see changes made in state protocols so that this issue can eventually be alleviated.

As the Lord put federal, state, and local investigators in our paths we learned about the insidious black market where infants from 0-3 years old are high commodities. We became aware of this absolutely evil issue of sex trafficking of infants and children under three. We were horrified to learn that babies were being bought and sold for sex and also for organ parts!

We learned that, in the past, women who were being sex trafficked used to have in-home abortions, now were being allowed to have their babies because they brought even more money. As we learned about these things, we realized that God had so much more for us to do – not just help rescue abandoned babes and help at risk mothers, but to advocate for infants and children 0-3 years of age who were victims of such heinous acts! We learned that there is no other government department or organization that solely advocates for children 0-3 years old in these areas. Since very young children cannot name their perpetrators and tell what has happened to them and because of the way laws are currently written, it is very difficult to bring perpetrators to justice. We felt that we must advocate for our most vulnerable citizens of Georgia. We are still proponents for the baby boxes, but our mission has shifted at this time. We believe we will at some point in the future, address the implementation of baby boxes in our state.

This was an amazing time of acceleration, as God moved us into many different avenues, connecting us with people of influence. We connected with other safe haven organizations and began to partner with them across the country. During this time, we researched and studied the many laws surrounding infant abandonment. Thankfully, we had many volunteers who assisted us in gathering mass amounts of information. We were able to meet with the original writer of Georgia's safe haven law. We began to see the need to revise the law, as it only afforded at-risk mothers seven days in which to relinquish parental rights without penalty. The only place that babies could be taken at that time were hospitals. So, we began working with state legislators to see about amending the law. Again, the Lord moved mightily and The Hope Box was able to work with legislators to revise the law and have it passed in one single session! We later learned this never happens. It usually takes years to get a law amended and passed – with God all things are possible! We will continue to champion for children ages 0-3, to work alongside our state and federal representatives, and to see that laws are written and revised to protect them.

> *"Learn to do good; seek justice, defend oppression. Take up the cause of the fatherless; plead the cause of the widow."*
>
> *Isaiah 1:17 NIV*

CHAPTER 10

The Hope Box Stories

Livyia's Story

Imagine being a scared seventeen-year-old high school girl, pregnant and in labor and too afraid to go to the hospital. Imagine Googling home births and delivering your baby in a bathtub, in secret, knowing if your father finds out, your baby will more than likely be sold, and you will be sent back to your foreign country. This is the real-life scenario of The Hope Box's first baby rescue. What could have been another tragic story on the local news of a baby being found abandoned, instead is a beautiful story of redemption. The mother not only Googled home births, but also Googled what to do with a baby you cannot keep and miraculously she found The Hope Box website. She called the hotline number and I answered. The rescue team went and met in the parking lot of a nearby church. We walked her through her options – whether she wanted to parent her child, choose adoption, or choose to enact the safe haven law. The mother explained to us that she could not parent her baby because it would place her and her baby in danger. So, she chose to give her baby up for adoption. She chose to do a private adoption. The Hope Box helped her find an adoption attorney who matched her baby with an a home study approved family. She was able to choose the family she wanted her baby to be adopted by. Baby Livyia was saved and delivered into the hands of a loving family, who had been praying for a child to adopt. Without The Hope Box this story could have ended much differently.

Chloe's Story

Baby Chloe was born to two loving immigrant parents living in the United States on work visas. She was very much wanted, and the parents were excited when the day of her arrival came; however, delivery complications ensued, and a vacuum extraction was used. During delivery, Baby Chloe sustained a head trauma due to a fractured skull. Her parents were torn. They loved their daughter but knew they would not be able to get the needed medical help necessary for her upon return to their home country. They researched on the internet what to do with an infant they could not care for and found The Hope Box. I met with them and explained their options. They were unaware they could choose for their child to be adopted, since adoption was not part of their culture. In their country, unwanted or sick female babies did not get the same care as male infants, and her condition only further complicated the potential for quality care. The parents decided to do a private adoption because they wanted to be able to continue to have contact with the adoptive family and with their baby. We were able to help the couple find an adoption attorney and a state approved family. The parents were shocked that someone would want their baby who had medical problems, but gladly signed over parental rights to the Roberts family. Don't get me wrong, this baby was so loved by both parents. It was the hardest thing in world for Chloe's birth mother to place her in someone else's arms, and even though she was putting her baby girl first, she was also giving away a piece of her own heart. Fortunately, it also was an answered prayer to the Roberts family who has been praying for a child for ten years.

The Roberts had been trying to have a child on their own for years but were unable to conceive. They made the decision to adopt and went through the lengthy process of completing a home study with the state. The biological parents chose them because they knew she would be loved and well cared for by this family who so desperately wanted to be parents. Unbelievably, Mrs. Roberts had suffered the same kind of head injury as a teenager and knew what medical care Chloe would need. Chloe received treatment and therapy for her injuries and received a clean bill of health right after her first birthday! The Roberts keep in contact with the biological parents, sending them pictures of Chloe and updating them about how she is doing. Again, The Hope Box was able to help a child not only find a forever family, but ultimately save her life!

Ella's Story

Baby Ella's birth mother knew she would be unable to care for her daughter. She knew she did not want her baby to go into the foster care system, as she had been a part of it as a child herself. Not sure what to do, she Googled and found The Hope Box. Our rescue team went to her in the hospital and explained her choices. She decided to do a private adoption, as she did not want to disclose as much detail as required in an adoption with an agency. We were able to connect her with a private attorney and then showed her a list of prospective parents who were home study approved. She chose the Banister family. The Banisters are the parents of three biological daughters who felt God had another child for them through adoption. They were beyond excited when I contacted them and asked if they would like to meet the biological mother of baby Ella. They immediately said yes, and within a short amount of time were at the hospital meeting their daughter. The mother fell in love with the couple and knew they were the ones she wanted her daughter to be raised by. She was happy to know that baby Ella would have three big sisters to love her, play with her, and teach her many things. The Banisters felt an immediate connection with the mother and agreed for the adoption to be open. The Banisters prayed with Allison asking the Lord to help her in the coming days and to bless her. Without The Hope Box, this mother could have made a different choice with a much different outcome.

A Trafficker's Story

We were contacted by a caseworker in a local hospital. She had an "uneasy" feeling about a situation that was happening with an at-risk mother and her newborn. Our rescue team went to the hospital to meet with the caseworker and the mother. When our team entered the room, we saw a beautiful young mom and another woman in the room who was not related to the mother. I asked the woman to leave so that I could speak privately with the mother. I explained to the mother who we (The Hope Box) were and told her we help mothers at-risk. I asked how we could help her. She began to tell me, "but you don't understand, I thought I was going to have my babies (twin girls) in jail, but I got out and then went into labor. I came here and this woman showed up and I do not know her." I realized that the young woman was in trafficking. I asked her how long she had been trafficked and she said, "my whole life." The young woman said that she believed the other woman was a madam or someone connected to trafficking, but she was too afraid to say anything to anyone at the hospital, thinking that she would get in trouble. The madam had signed all of the paperwork, including the birth certificates for the babies. She matched all of the babies' information as if she were the babies' mother! I immediately asked the mother if I could notify the hospital of what was going on and she said yes. The mother was moved to another room and the hospital was put on lock down. The hospital was able to correct all of the documentation including the birth certificates. After explaining to this young woman her options, she chose to do an adoption with an agency. The hospital was very grateful that The Hope Box interceded in the situation and they filed a police report concerning the stranger. If The Hope Box had not been called, the babies would have been kidnapped by a madam and would more than likely have been sex trafficked. The mother chose adoption through an agency a week later.

Sarah Koeppen

The Judge's Grace

I received a frantic call on our hotline one day from a foster parent who was concerned for the safety of an infant in her care. The infant's mother was a prostitute and was taking the infant to hotels with her while "working." DFCS became aware of the situation and the baby was placed in foster care. The biological mother messaged the foster parent and said that she was coming to get her baby. She told the foster parent, "my pimp says I can get a lot of money for my baby." Since the baby had not been trafficked *yet*, the police could do nothing – no crime had occurred, but because the foster parent contacted The Hope Box, we were able to contact the courts and a judge. The judge was able to get a court order to protect the child so that the mother could not have access to the child. The foster parent was eventually able to adopt the baby!

Because no crime had happened yet, police nor DFCS were able to do anything to protect this infant – laws need to be changed! When laws were written in the past, no one could even conceive of the sex trafficking of infants, thus the laws do not adequately protect infants and children three years and younger. The Hope Box is currently and actively working alongside representatives to see these laws changed so that our most defenseless and precious babies can be better protected.

Hotline Story

One night, we received a call on our hotline number from a woman who lived in another state. She was a nurse and she was concerned about an infant in her apartment complex. She heard a baby crying a few doors down from her and she knew that a couple lived there, and the woman was pregnant. She was also aware of drug activity in that apartment. She was concerned that the mother and infant were not in the hospital. It bothered her all day while she was working. When she got off work, she contacted The Hope Box. I asked her if she'd ever met the couple and she said yes. I told her to keep me on the phone and go and knock on the door and just say you are checking on them, and that you'd heard a baby crying. When the nurse asked how they were doing, they just motioned in the apartment to a corner and said, "it's in the back". The mother and her partner were in the bed getting high and the baby was wrapped up in a dirty blanket. The baby was not moving, and the nurse was very scared that it was dead, but then it moved! I told her to pick it up and to tell the parents that the baby needed medical care. The mom said, "just get rid of it." The nurse stayed on the line with me as she drove to the ER with the baby in her lap. We called the hospital to let them know that an infant was being brought in and that the safe haven law had been invoked by the mother. A couple of hours later the hospital called The Hope Box to let us know that the infant was stable and that DFCS had been contacted. Thank God for this good Samaritan nurse who listened to her gut and acted on behalf of this precious baby! Without her willingness to reach out to The Hope Box this infant more than likely would have died!

Not all of our rescues end in adoption. Many times, they end with mothers finding out they are not alone and with the help from The Hope Box and other local resources, are able to choose to keep their babies and parent them. We are so thankful when this happens! Our ultimate goal, for any child, is that he or she is able to stay with his or her birth mother and be nurtured and cared for by the biological family. We have had opportunities to assist at-risk mothers so that they are able to parent their infants.

A Young Mother's Story

A young mother contacted us because she had lost her job and had nowhere to live. She had no support system to rely on (family or friends). The Hope Box was able to get her a hotel room so that she and her baby were not sleeping in her car. We were able to get her resources for the baby (diapers, formula, etc.) and also a stable place to live.

A Story of Domestic Violence

Another mother contacted us, thinking she wanted to invoke the safe haven law for her unborn baby. Pregnant, she had recently fled from another state because of domestic violence. She had two older children but had nothing she needed for the baby. She had literally left everything behind. When I asked her if she wanted to parent this baby, she said, "yes, but how can I? I don't have anything!" The Hope Box was able to get her the needed items for the baby. A few weeks later, this mother delivered a healthy baby girl. Baby is doing well, her mother, is now working, and her two older siblings are enjoying their new school and home.

A Story of Homelessness

We recently had a homeless mother of three young children contact us. She and her children were sleeping in the back of a moving van. The mother had been in a shelter but left because her daughter had been molested there. We met with her and her kids at a Waffle House. We fed the kids and mom and explained her different options. This mother wants her children to be safe and off the streets. She had not reached out to DFCS because she didn't want her children to be in the system and to be separated from one another. All of her children are older, so the safe haven law was not an option for her, but we did discuss adoption. This mother is considering adoption, but currently has opted to let her children go with other family members for now. The Hope Box was able to get her children in a hotel for the night until the children could go with other family members. We don't know if we'll hear back from her again but our prayers are with her and her three children!

These are just a few of The Hope Box stories. Each one is unique, but at the core of every story is an at-risk mother and her child(ren) who needed someone to advocate for them. The Hope Box is grateful to be able to walk alongside these women and help them make life altering decisions that change the course of their lives for the better.

> *"Jesus looked at them and said, "With man this is impossible, but with God all things are possible."*
> *Matthew 19:26 NIV*

CHAPTER 11

What's on the Horizon for The Hope Box

The Hope Box will continue to work in the state of Georgia to help rescue abandoned babies and assist at-risk mothers with making the best decisions for their futures as well as their babies' futures. Our hope and goal are to have regional offices throughout the state so that all 159 counties in Georgia will have Hope Box representatives, and we will see baby abandonment as a thing of the past in our state. Georgia is just the beginning; we believe eventually The Hope Box will be nationwide. As a nation we have some of the highest statistics of abandonment, abuse and neglect amongst ages 0-3. We are the United States of America, not a third world county – this should not be the case! Our most vulnerable citizens deserve protection and care. The Hope Box dream is to see these national statistics, regarding abandonment, abuse, and neglect for ages 0-3, significantly decrease. There is need for reform in the area of child welfare in our country and the Department of Family and Children's Services are in great need of a major overhaul. In the United States, more than four children die from child abuse and neglect ***on a daily basis.*** Over seventy percent of these children are below the age of three. Boys and girls become victims at nearly the same rate. 2.9 million cases of child abuse are reported every year in the United States. The highest rate of child abuse in children under the age of one is 25.3% per 1,000. Almost five children die every day from child abuse and 71.8% of all child fatalities were younger than three years old. 49.6% of children who die from child abuse are under one year old. We know that 22,000 infants where abandoned in hospitals just last year in this country (American Society for the Positive Care of Children website, americanspcc.org). This number is probably even higher, since children this age have very limited if any communicative skills. The Hope

Box is the answer to many of the problems that plague those systems. By joining hands with other non-profit and governmental agencies and sharing resources and information to collectively work as a team, we feel that infant abandonment and abuse can be greatly reduced, with the goal of total alleviation. The Hope Box also has a heart to see laws concerning child abandonment and abuse changed nationally. We have worked in our state to see changes made and we hope to see those changes made at the national level as well. We welcome conversations with government leaders and agencies at state and national levels. Our heart is to continue to go through every open door that is presented before us as we continue the journey of The Hope Box.

> *"The King will reply, "Truly I tell you, whatever you did for one of the least of these brothers and sisters of mine, you did for me."*
> *Matthew 25:40 NIV*

CHAPTER 12

Epilogue

I am a mother, a wife, and a Christ follower. I did not know what my life would look like, but I certainly never dreamed it would be like this! As I reflect on how all of *this* became a reality, I am truly amazed – God is forever surprising me! When you look at my qualifications on paper, I should not have been able to do the things that I have done – but God! I am just crazy enough to believe God and be obedient to what He has put on my heart. Getting up every day and making phone calls, sending emails, and meeting with leaders and asking them to stand with me in protecting infants in our state, and sometimes nothing happens. Only to do it again and again. Is it worth it? YES! Because what we do MATTERS!

What The Hope Box does changes lives and changes destinies. It is the heartbeat that is going to change this nation when it comes to protecting infants and children!

So many times we get lost feeling things are so impossible, instead of walking into the impossible and watching things become possible. I experienced many hurts as people who I admired and looked up to told me that what I felt God wanted me to do was impossible – to create The Hope Box. I had to choose to believe what God said over the words of others. I had to stand in who He says I am not what others say about me. I had to believe in my identity and the call on my life. That it is greater than what others have said about me. I had to choose not to walk in offense but allow those words to strengthen my resolve and not weaken my position. When God tells me to move, I move – even when I don't understand it, when I am embarrassed about it, or complain about it – I believe all things work together for good for those that love the Lord. I want my legacy to be a legacy of hope. I am thankful for those in my life who gave me my *yes* when I shared God's vision and plan for The Hope Box. I hope this book gives you your *YES*! And I hope you understand the vital role you play in making this world a better place!!

FINAL NOTE

Our son Elijah became an official *Koeppen* in the spring of 2020! After ten years of legally being our son, he chose to change his last name to Koeppen. Elijah is the heartbeat that started The Hope Box, and only fitting that the end of this book *coincidentally* coincided with this wonderful event! We love you Elijah Koeppen!

> **"And who knows but that you have come to your royal position for such a time as this?"**
> **Esther 4:14b NIV**

Printed in the United States
By Bookmasters